CALM

— FOR —

EVERY DAY

Simple Tips and Inspiring
Quotes to Help You Find Peace

vie

CALM FOR EVERY DAY

This edition copyright © Summersdale Publishers Ltd, 2022
First edition published as *The Little Book of Calm*, 2018

Illustrations © Romanova Ekaterina/Shutterstock.com

An Hachette UK Company
www.hachette.co.uk

Vie Books, an imprint of Summersdale Publishers Ltd
Part of Octopus Publishing Group Limited
Carmelite House
50 Victoria Embankment
LONDON
EC4Y 0DZ
UK

www.summersdale.com

Printed and bound in China

ISBN: 978-1-80007-182-7

Substantial discounts on bulk quantities of Summersdale books are available to corporations, professional associations and other organizations. For details contact general enquiries: telephone: +44 (0) 1243 771107 or email: enquiries@summersdale.com.

INTRODUCTION

On the face of it, being calm might seem to be the ability to handle all situations – but this isn't quite true. Nobody is immune to the feelings of worry, anxiety or concern. In fact, these feelings are a normal and vital part of the human experience. Instead, being calm is all about how you deal with these feelings. You may be anxious, but this needn't throw you into a tailspin. With a few techniques and practices, anybody can learn to be calm. This little book will help you to manage yourself and your emotions, keep you thinking clearly, and help you to live a calmer, more contented life.

WITHIN YOU THERE IS
A STILLNESS AND A
SANCTUARY TO WHICH
YOU CAN RETREAT AT ANY
TIME AND BE YOURSELF.

Hermann Hesse

LEARN TO BE CALM
AND YOU WILL
ALWAYS BE HAPPY.

Paramahansa Yogananda

THE BENEFITS OF BEING CALM

Being able to bring a sense of calm into your life has no end of benefits for both your body and mind. Calmness is good for you – stress and prolonged tension are harmful to your body in the long term, so being able to manage these feelings helps to keep you healthy. You will be able to focus more fully, as being calm allows you to give matters your whole attention without distraction,

and you're more likely to make informed, rational decisions. And, without the frantic feeling of stress, you are free to live in the moment. You can savour the food you eat, immerse yourself in a book or a film, and notice the wonderful details of the world around you. With the ability to find calm, you will live a clearer, richer and more vibrant life.

ADOPT THE PACE OF NATURE: HER SECRET IS PATIENCE.

Ralph Waldo Emerson

IF YOU CHANGE
YOUR MIND, YOU CAN
CHANGE YOUR LIFE.

Michelle Williams

JUST BREATHE

If you're feeling stressed, one of the
first steps to unwinding is making
yourself slow down. To do this, try a
simple breathing exercise. Sit or stand
somewhere where you are comfortable,
and relax your body. Breathe in through
your nose and let your body fill with
as much air as it can comfortably hold.
Then slowly exhale through your mouth.
This will soothe the immediate feelings
of anxiety that can bubble up and will
help you to focus on your next step.

IF WE DO EACH THING
CALMLY AND CAREFULLY
WE WILL GET IT DONE
QUICKER AND WITH
MUCH LESS STRESS.

Viggo Mortensen

ALLOW YOURSELF PEACE

If you consider everything that's going through your mind – from the big worries to the mundane everyday – you may be surprised at how many are introduced by societal pressures or "manufactured" worries. While it's natural to be concerned about the essentials in life, such as safe living conditions or mental and physical health, other worries – like what other people may think of you – come from the pressures of our society. We often look for things that we can be negative about when we would be much healthier and happier if we were able to let our worries go. In that way, learning to calm yourself is an important skill, enabling you to be more appreciative of life's pleasures. We often allow stress and fatigue to obscure the beauty there is all around us; when we are calm and centred, it is much easier to appreciate all that is good in life and steer away from external pressures.

SET PEACE OF MIND AS
YOUR HIGHEST GOAL,
AND ORGANIZE YOUR
LIFE AROUND IT.

Brian Tracy

STOP TRYING TO
DEFINE WHO YOU ARE
AND JUST BE.

Cara Delevingne

READ THE SIGNS

Being able to maintain calm in your life is all about how you're able to manage stress and difficult situations, so one of the most important things to practise is recognizing when you are getting stressed. Stress will affect everybody in a different way, but some common symptoms are feeling overwhelmed or irritable, having racing thoughts or difficulty concentrating, or having physical symptoms such as headaches, dizziness, muscle tension, changes to

your appetite or fatigue. The more aware you are of when you get stressed, the better you will be able to deal with your feelings. You may also find it helpful to keep a diary of the things that make you anxious or tense. You might notice a pattern forming – perhaps you get anxious when you go to a particular place or when you have to speak in public, for instance. Once you know what triggers your negative feelings, you can begin to take steps to deal with them.

HE WHO LIVES IN
HARMONY WITH HIMSELF
LIVES IN HARMONY
WITH THE UNIVERSE.

Marcus Aurelius

LET YOUR SOUL
STAND COOL AND
COMPOSED BEFORE A
MILLION UNIVERSES.

Walt Whitman

PRACTISE MEDITATION FOR A CALM MIND

When you practise meditation, your mind is not focused on what's around you, or on the things that are concerning you. It is the art of allowing your mind to become completely still, like a pool of water with no ripples. To begin, find a quiet, uncluttered place and sit in a comfortable position. Close your eyes if you would like. Take slow, steady breaths and focus your attention on them. If a thought comes into your mind, acknowledge it

but don't pursue it. Remain focused on your breathing. Notice if any parts of your body feel tense – if so, relax them. Let yourself be still and soft. Do this for as long as you would like to, whether that's for five minutes or for half an hour. Emptying your mind is easier said than done, and some people find it easier to reach that state of calm than others. However, with practice, anybody can master meditation and reap the benefits.

"MEDITATION AND PRAYING CHANGE YOUR SPIRIT INTO SOMETHING POSITIVE. IF IT IS ALREADY POSITIVE, IT MAKES IT BETTER.

Tina Turner

IN MEDITATION,
I CAN LET GO OF
EVERYTHING.

Hugh Jackman

FIVE-MINUTE MEDITATION

You don't have to clear your schedule to make time for meditation. As long as you have a few minutes and a quiet space to sit in, you can meditate whenever you like. Once you're comfortable in your space, set a timer so that you don't have to watch the clock, then meditate until your time is up. Try this if you have a few minutes before leaving the house or some time to spare at the end of your lunch break. Even just five minutes of stillness and calm breathing can set you up for the rest of the day.

FOREVER IS COMPOSED OF NOWS.

Emily Dickinson

MINDFULNESS ON THE GO

If you're out and about, practising mindfulness is another technique you can try as it helps to bring your focus away from your anxiety and into the here and now. Pick any object in your surroundings and concentrate on its shape and texture in order to block out other distractions. You could focus on the flame of a candle, a vase of flowers or, if you're not at home, something in front of you: your bag, or a rock on the ground, for example. Look at

your chosen object with your eyes fully open or partially closed, and let yourself relax into your gaze. Notice all the tiny details about what's in front of you – whether it's the pattern on its surface, tiny scratches or scuff marks, or the shape of its edges. Focusing intently on one object will keep your mind in the present moment and give your body a chance to unwind from whatever tension you are experiencing.

MEDITATION AND BEING CLOSE TO YOURSELF HELPS EVERYTHING IN YOUR LIFE.

Liv Tyler

IF YOU JUST SIT AND
OBSERVE, YOU WILL SEE
HOW RESTLESS YOUR
MIND IS... BUT OVER TIME
IT DOES CALM AND...
YOU START TO SEE
THINGS MORE CLEARLY.

Steve Jobs

COUNT ON IT

If you find it tricky to keep your mind still whilst meditating, try using numbers as an anchor. Rather than trying not to think, using numbers allows you to redirect your thoughts instead, as they are something neutral to focus on. As you breathe, count slowly to 100 in your head. If your thoughts wander while you do this just bring them back to the counts. Do this as many times as you need to: gradually your mind will become quieter.

IT'S DIFFICULT TO DESCRIBE THE EFFECT IT'S HAD ON MY LIFE. I CAN ONLY MENTION MAYBE A FEW WORDS: CALM, CLARITY, A BALANCE.

Martin Scorsese on meditation

GIVE YOGA A GO

Yoga is an excellent way to alleviate any feelings of anxiety. Combining elements of meditation, stretching and gentle exercise, it's an activity that both strengthens your body and calms your mind. There are many different types of yoga to try – look up classes in your local area or, if you'd rather practise in the comfort of your own home, buy DVDs or find instructional videos online.

DO SOME YOGA.
I NEVER FEEL MORE
BEAUTIFUL THAN AFTER
I'VE REALLY SPENT
SOME TIME BREATHING.

Olivia Wilde

USE THE WORLD AROUND YOU

Use your environment to help cultivate a sense of peace and tranquillity. Venture outside for some fresh air, find a green space and use natural outdoor surroundings as a calming influence. A silent space can also do wonders for your state of mind – whether it's a room in your house, somewhere at work or even a bathroom cubicle, retreating from noise even for a few minutes gives your mind and your nerves a chance to unwind.

BEING OUTDOORS,
LISTENING TO THE WORLD
WAKE UP AROUND ME,
I SHED ALL THE STRESS
THAT COMES WITH MY JOB.

Chris Pratt

SOOTHE AWAY WORRIES WITH MANTRAS

A mantra is a short word or phrase that you can say to help centre yourself. They're often used in meditation as repeating the sounds helps to bring your mind into a calmer, clearer state, but they can be used at any time. They can also be used for all manner of situations: to help you to control anger, to motivate you, to boost your self-confidence or, in this case, to bring you calm. Some phrases you might want to try are:

- I breathe in; I breathe out
- Just keep going
- All is well
- This feeling will pass

At stressful moments, say these to yourself quietly and slowly, close your eyes if you would like and slow your breathing. By doing so, you will interrupt your feelings of stress and bring yourself back to the present moment. Saying a mantra can also be soothing, and you will be a voice of comfort to yourself.

I USE BREATH TO CONNECT
ME TO THE PRESENT
MOMENT AND TO CREATE
SPACE IN MY BODY.

Tracee Ellis Ross

AFTER A STORM
COMES A CALM.

Proverb

PROGRESSIVE RELAXATION

When we're anxious our bodies often tense up without us realizing. Progressive relaxation can be a good way of releasing this tension. Start by sitting or lying down. Focus on one muscle group – one hand, for instance. On an inhale, tense it as hard as you can for five seconds. As you exhale, release the tension until that muscle group is limp. Take your time and repeat this for all the muscle groups in your body. Not only is this exercise relaxing, but it helps you to become aware of what tension feels like in your body.

WHO YOU ARE IS
WHO YOU ARE RIGHT
THIS SECOND, NOT
WHO YOU WERE AT ANY
MOMENT IN THE PAST.

Thandiwe Newton

WRITE IT OUT

Many people find that keeping a diary is a helpful tool to combat feelings of uneasiness and stress. The act of writing can be therapeutic as it helps to put some distance between you and your thoughts. A diary could take any form – it could be anything from a bullet list of things that are on your mind to long entries where you're able to muse about everything you're thinking. You

don't have to write in it every day, and
you don't even have to write on paper.
You could type it onto a computer
or a phone or email yourself instead.
Next time you're tense, try putting
pen to paper (or fingers to keyboard)
and write down what's concerning you,
as this will help to clear your head
and give you a new perspective.

ONE OFTEN CALMS ONE'S GRIEF BY RECOUNTING IT.

Pierre Corneille

IF EVERYTHING WAS
PERFECT, YOU WOULD
NEVER LEARN AND YOU
WOULD NEVER GROW.

Beyoncé

CHOOSE TO MOVE!

Exercise is not only good for your body – it's good for your mind too! Getting out and moving your body releases serotonin, the "happy hormone", which is both a mood booster and a stress buster. Running is a great exercise to get tension out of your system, and the rhythm of your feet on the pavement can be therapeutic. If you'd prefer something gentler, swimming has a soothing rhythm to it as well, and in focusing on your strokes you can lull yourself into a calmer mindset. Even something as simple as walking is beneficial and easy to incorporate into your day. Try walking to work or taking a 20-minute stroll in your lunch break, for instance. However you choose to move, being more active will help you to relax in your downtime, sleep better and increase positivity, all of which will ultimately help you feel calmer.

RUNNING REALLY
HELPS ME CLEAR MY
HEAD AND MAKES ME
FEEL GOOD, ESPECIALLY
WHEN I'M STRESSED.

Katie Holmes

I GO TO NATURE TO BE SOOTHED AND HEALED, AND TO HAVE MY SENSES PUT IN ORDER.

John Burroughs

MAKE TIME FOR SELF-CARE

Self-care is anything that you do to help to protect or nurture your own health and well-being. Taking the time for self-care in your day-to-day life is a big step toward keeping yourself happy, healthy and stress free. Acts of self-care can be anything from keeping up mundane everyday tasks – like brushing your teeth twice a day, doing the washing-up or shopping for groceries – to making sure you take time out to make

yourself feel good – such as indulging in a long bath, calling a friend for a chat, or taking your whole lunch break to go for a walk or read a book instead of spending it at your desk. The small things are just as important as the bigger things in keeping you balanced and feeling well, and it's at the times when you feel most pressured that you need to remember this the most.

YOU HAVE TO TAKE
EACH MOMENT
AS IT COMES.

Benedict Cumberbatch

THE ORDINARY ACTS WE
PRACTISE EVERY DAY
AT HOME ARE OF MORE
IMPORTANCE TO THE SOUL
THAN THEIR SIMPLICITY
MIGHT SUGGEST.

Thomas Moore

PUT YOUR THOUGHTS TO
SLEEP, DO NOT LET THEM
CAST A SHADOW OVER
THE MOON OF YOUR HEART.
LET GO OF THINKING.

Rumi

BE HAPPY FOR THIS
MOMENT. THIS MOMENT
IS YOUR LIFE.

Omar Khayyam

PRACTISE PATIENCE

Being calm has a lot to do with being patient. When we're impatient, our stress levels can go from 0–60 in seconds and these feelings can go on to affect us long after the event has passed. But patience is a skill and like any skill it can be practised. Try saving an episode of a TV show until the weekend, choosing a longer line to wait in in the supermarket or waiting 20 minutes before eating a tasty treat. By gradually acclimatizing yourself to waiting you will improve your ability to stay cool and collected when it matters.

HE THAT CAN HAVE PATIENCE CAN HAVE WHAT HE WILL.

Benjamin Franklin

STRETCH

Something as simple as stretching for 30 seconds can be a really effective stress-buster. Performing regular stretches helps to relieve muscle tension (which, if left to build up, can lead to headaches) and it's excellent for your circulation which will help you to think more clearly too. Try a shoulder stretch: raise your arms above your head, lock your fingers and turn your palms so they're facing upward. Try to stretch your hands up while keeping your shoulders down. Hold this for a few breaths before bringing your hands down again. Or you could try a stretch to open your chest. Stand up with your feet hip-width apart and look straight ahead. Clasp your hands behind you and then lift them as high as you can. This stretch is particularly good if you spend a lot of time at a computer or desk as it counteracts the effects of hunching over a screen.

MEDITATION CAN HELP US
EMBRACE OUR WORRIES,
OUR FEAR, OUR ANGER; AND
THAT IS VERY HEALING.

Thích Nhất Hạnh

CONTROL WHAT YOU CAN, BUT FLOW WITH WHAT YOU CAN'T.

Alan Cohen

GIVE YOURSELF
A HAND MASSAGE

Try giving yourself a hand massage for some calming therapy on the go. Start by sitting comfortably and deepen your breathing. Place your left hand in your lap, palm up, then hold it with your right hand – the right thumb should be on top of your palm. Press your thumb into your palm and move it in small circular movements around the edge of your hand, spending extra time around the joints of your fingers. Take as long as you need. Repeat on the other hand when you're ready.

TO THE MIND
THAT IS STILL, THE
WHOLE UNIVERSE
SURRENDERS.

Lao Tzu

I AM MY OWN
SANCTUARY.

Lady Gaga

BELIEVE THAT LIFE IS
WORTH LIVING AND
YOUR BELIEF WILL HELP
CREATE THE FACT.

William James

POSITIVE CHANGE

If you're feeling stuck in a rut, why not try something new? Getting involved in a new hobby or activity is a great way to shift your perspective. You could try joining a gym, signing up to a yoga, Pilates or martial arts course, learning another language or the basics of photography at the local college, or

knitting an enormous blanket. Whatever you choose to do, having a project to get your teeth into gives you focus and takes your mind off your problems. Evening classes and courses are also a good way to meet new people – and remember, everyone is in the same boat, so try to relax and enjoy it.

I'M A BIG BELIEVER THAT
LIFE CHANGES AS MUCH
AS YOU WANT IT TO.

Martin Freeman

HAVE PATIENCE WITH
ALL THINGS, BUT
CHIEFLY HAVE PATIENCE
WITH YOURSELF.

St Francis de Sales

PUZZLE IT OUT

Although relaxation techniques are useful, sometimes all that's needed to bring you some calm is a little distraction. Puzzles are a good way to take your mind off your worries and absorb it in something else. Try crosswords, Sudoku, brain-teasers, jigsaws or quizzes to give your mind a break as well as a workout!

WHEN SOMETHING FEELS
HEAVY, BREAK IT DOWN
UNTIL ONE PIECE OF IT
IS LIGHT ENOUGH TO
HANDLE. BEGIN THERE.

Bernie Siegel

GOOD FOOD,
GOOD MOOD

Your diet is another important factor in helping you feel balanced, and eating the right things can have a hugely positive effect on your mood. Eating three meals a day at regularly spaced intervals will maintain your blood sugar levels and keep you from feeling hungry and irritable. Eating at least five portions of fruit and vegetables a day is important too, as these will give you the right vitamins to help your brain function at its best. Vitamins B and C are particularly useful and can be found in citrus fruits and leafy vegetables. Avoid making salty and sugary foods into a habit, as these don't nourish your body and can lead to health problems in the long run. In addition, try to minimize your alcohol consumption as it is a depressant and can disturb your sleep. Don't feel you have to cut these elements out of your diet but, to take the best care of your body and mind, enjoy them in moderation!

NOURISH TO FLOURISH

Make sure you're getting the right nutrients to keep your body and mind on top form. Magnesium is essential, particularly as it helps you to get better quality sleep. It can be found in spinach, broccoli, beans and oats. Protein is another key nutrient as it helps your brain to absorb tryptophan – the amino acid needed for the production of serotonin (the "happy hormone"). It can be found in chicken, fish, eggs, soya beans, chickpeas and many nuts and seeds. A balanced diet provides the body with all these key nutrients and more.

TENSION IS WHO YOU
THINK YOU SHOULD
BE. RELAXATION IS
WHO YOU ARE.

Chinese proverb

AROMATHERAPY

Essential oils have long been used to help calm the mind and body. It is believed that inhaling the smells from essential oils affects the hypothalamus, the part of the brain that controls the glands and hormones, thereby changing a person's mood and lowering their stress levels. To reap the benefits of aromatherapy oils, add a few drops onto a tissue and inhale or add a few drops to your bath and enjoy the soothing scent

as you soak. You could also give yourself a massage: incorporate a couple of drops of oil into a small amount of coconut, almond or olive oil and apply it directly to your skin. Some uplifting essential oils include chamomile, lavender and rose, and stimulating oils include black pepper, peppermint and rosemary. However, be aware that if you are using essential oils for the first time it is advisable to consult your doctor first.

WHERE THERE'S
PEACE, ALLOW
IT TO REIGN.

Chidera Eggerue

THE TIME TO RELAX
IS WHEN YOU DON'T
HAVE TIME FOR IT.

Sydney J. Harris

MAKE A TO-DO LIST

The feeling of having too much to do is one of the most common causes of stress. Whether you're in the workplace or at home, writing down a to-do list is the first step to feeling back in control. Take a piece of paper or type into your phone every task you can think of that needs doing. Sometimes just seeing the list of things can make you feel more at ease. However, if you're still feeling overwhelmed, organize the items on your list by priority. You might have a lot to do but perhaps only one or two items need doing today, and the rest can wait until tomorrow or a few days from now. Having a list and breaking it up into sections will give you a clearer picture of what needs doing – and make tackling it a lot more manageable.

WE MUST LET GO OF
THE LIFE WE HAVE
PLANNED, SO AS TO
ACCEPT THE ONE THAT
IS WAITING FOR US.

Joseph Campbell

NOTHING CAN BRING YOU PEACE BUT YOURSELF.

Ralph Waldo Emerson

TIDY IN 30 SECONDS

There's no need to deep clean the house every weekend, but keeping things clean around your home can have a huge effect on how you feel. Take an extra 30 seconds to wipe down the counter or the hob after cooking or always make your bed before you leave the house. Getting into the habit of doing these tiny acts will keep your home neat around the edges and keep you feeling comfortable and relaxed.

TO EVERY PROBLEM
THERE IS ALREADY A
SOLUTION, WHETHER
YOU KNOW IT OR NOT.

Grenville Kleiser

ORGANIZE YOURSELF

Creating order in your environment can help to create the feeling in your mind too. We all know the frustration of not being able to find that piece of correspondence or a particular piece of clothing. By bringing organization into your home you can minimize your stress and also enjoy the soothing effect of feeling more in control. Decluttering is

a good way to bring about this sense of order. Go through your desk, your kitchen drawers, your wardrobe or your garden shed and get rid of all the things you no longer use, want or need. Don't feel you have to do the whole house all at once – even decluttering one area of a room can make you feel calmer and more organized.

LIVE IN EACH SEASON AS
IT PASSES; BREATHE THE
AIR, DRINK THE DRINK,
TASTE THE FRUIT.

Henry David Thoreau

WHEREVER YOU ARE,
BE ALL THERE.

Jim Elliot

ORGANIZE YOUR WARDROBE

Sometimes one of the most difficult parts of the day is deciding what to wear! So take away some of the stress by making sure your wardrobe is organized. Declutter by donating or throwing out the things that you don't wear, and make room for the things you do. Organize what remains by item – tops, trousers, dresses, etc. Tidying your clothes will ensure you know where they are, which makes choosing outfits quick and easy, leaving you with one less thing to think about.

SMILE, BREATHE
AND GO SLOWLY.

Thích Nhất Hạnh

GET OUT OF YOUR HEAD
AND GET INTO YOUR HEART.
THINK LESS, FEEL MORE.

Osho

CALMNESS IS THE
CRADLE OF POWER.

J. G. Holland

LEARN TO SWITCH OFF

Watching TV can be a great way to relax and unwind but, as with most indulgences, it's important to enjoy it in moderation. On average we watch four hours of TV a day – such a huge drain on your time can lead to you feeling frustrated and unfulfilled in the long term. To keep a balance in your life, try to plan what you want to watch before turning on the TV, and don't let it take the place of spending time with loved ones or keeping up with your hobbies.

OUR JOB AS ADULTS IS TO BE THAT PARENT, TO BE THAT CARETAKER FOR OURSELVES. WE CAN'T REALLY LOOK FOR THAT NURTURING, FOR THAT CALM... FROM EXTERNAL SOURCES.

Jonathan Van Ness

SCREENS AWAY

It's not just the TV screen we should be mindful of. Any kind of screen that you spend time in front of – whether it's a phone, a tablet or a games console – is something to keep tabs on. Screens can be the cause of tension headaches if you focus on them for too long, and the light they emit can affect your sleep patterns. Plus, the time we spend on computers and phones can often reduce the time we spend interacting face-to-face with others. All these habits can leave us feeling uneasy and unhealthy in both body and mind. To combat this, make sure to take regular breaks if you work at a computer screen, and try to reduce your time with tech as much as possible. Making time for conversation with your partner or friends, or taking up a hobby, can help you to get away from a screen. You will feel physically better and more calm and composed.

A CONTENTED MIND
IS THE GREATEST
BLESSING A MAN CAN
ENJOY IN THIS WORLD.

Joseph Addison

EVERYTHING YOU CAN
DO CAN BE DONE
BETTER FROM A PLACE
OF RELAXATION.

Stephen C. Paul

TACKLE MONEY MATTERS

If money worries are weighing on your mind, taking back control of the matter is the first step. Create a spreadsheet showing all your monthly outgoings and don't miss anything out. Then go over areas where you could save money. Do you have the best possible energy tariff, for example? Research this using price comparison sites to work out how your prices compare to others. And how much food do you throw away each week? If this is a problem, plan your meals for a week before you shop to minimize waste.

CULTIVATE PEACE.
COMMIT TO PEACE.
INSIST ON IT.

Melody Beattie

TALK IT OUT

If you're feeling tied up in knots by a tough decision or a difficult situation, try turning to a family member or friend. Call them up to chat, or arrange to meet up and spend a while talking to them about how you feel. Your companion will be able to offer you comfort and support. Vocalizing your thoughts can be cathartic, helping to take a weight off your mind and see your situation from a fresh perspective.

IT'S EASIER
TO BE BRAVE WHEN
YOU'RE NOT ALONE.

Amy Poehler

SLEEP EASY

On the other side of a good night's sleep, life's difficulties and challenges can seem a little less stressful than they otherwise would. You feel better and can think more clearly and this is because sleep is the body's way of recharging itself, both physically and mentally. To help you get the best night's sleep you can, keep your room as a sanctuary – a place where you come only to rest. Associating the room with sleep and relaxation will make it easier to leave your worries

behind. If you still find yourself tossing and turning once you've gone to bed, try not to dwell on it. Studies have shown that worrying about not getting enough sleep is one of the biggest factors in preventing us from sleeping! Most people will have no problem functioning with six or seven hours' sleep, and if you have lost sleep, you only need to catch up on about a third of the lost time to get back to normal.

QUIET YOUR MIND, BREATHE AND LET GO OF WORDS, WORRY AND PLANS.

Doreen Virtue

WE'RE USED TO BEING SUFFOCATED. WE NEED TO SIT, BE KIND TO OURSELVES, AND JUST LOOK INSIDE FOR A MINUTE.

Michaela Coel

PREPARE YOUR MIND FOR SLEEP

Practise being able to clear your head before you sleep. You don't have to completely empty your mind, but the goal is to be able to put your thoughts to one side before you hit the pillow, leaving you free to sink into sleep without being pestered by an overburdened brain. To do this, try writing down how you're feeling in a journal or diary, or making a to-do list for the next day. You could also talk to a friend or family member to help ease your mind. Devising a bedtime routine can also help to let your body know when it's time to sleep. This might involve having a bath followed by a hot drink, or reading a chapter of a book. You could even work in a meditation exercise or a bedtime yoga sequence to your routine. Eventually, these regular pre-bedtime activities will act as triggers and tell your body and mind to switch off and go to sleep.

PEACE IS NOT MERELY
A DISTANT GOAL THAT
WE SEEK BUT A MEANS
BY WHICH WE ARRIVE
AT THAT GOAL.

Martin Luther King Jr

A FREE MIND IS ONE
WHICH IS UNTROUBLED
AND UNFETTERED
BY ANYTHING.

Meister Eckhart

ONE THING AT A TIME

If you're feeling overwhelmed, choose
one thing from your to-do list and
focus your whole attention on it. Ignore
any interruptions – whether that's by
turning off email notifications, switching
off your phone or taking yourself into
another room. No matter how many
other things you have to do, don't begin
another task until you've finished what
you started. By giving yourself space
and time, and by completing the job,
you will regain your sense of control.

SOMETIMES THE
SMALLEST STEP IN THE
RIGHT DIRECTION ENDS
UP BEING THE BIGGEST
STEP OF YOUR LIFE.

Emma Stone

LAUGH OUT LOUD

Laughter is the best medicine, or so the saying goes... but it's true! And it might just be one of the best ways to combat feelings of stress. Laughter relaxes your body, gives your immune system a boost, increases blood flow – and it triggers the release of endorphins, the chemicals that make you feel good. So tune in to some comedy or have a good giggle with a friend to give yourself a boost.

KEEP SMILING, BECAUSE LIFE IS A BEAUTIFUL THING AND THERE'S SO MUCH TO SMILE ABOUT.

Marilyn Monroe

YOUR MIND WILL ANSWER
MOST QUESTIONS IF YOU
LEARN TO RELAX AND
WAIT FOR THE ANSWER.

William S. Burroughs

VERY LITTLE IS NEEDED
TO MAKE A HAPPY LIFE;
IT IS ALL WITHIN
YOURSELF, IN YOUR
WAY OF THINKING.

Marcus Aurelius

LET YOUR WORRIES FLOAT AWAY

Visualization can be a powerful tool when it comes to bringing you a sense of calm. If your mind is racing, and particularly if your worries start circling round your mind at night, first tell yourself, "I can't do anything practical to help this now – I can think about it in the morning." Visualize a hot air balloon, and picture your worry inside the basket. Then watch it float away into the distance, taking your anxieties far away above the clouds and out of your mind.

YOU CANNOT PERCEIVE
BEAUTY BUT WITH
A SERENE MIND.

Henry David Thoreau

CRACK A SMILE

Often the last thing you feel like doing if you're going through a difficult time is smiling. But the act of smiling can be the key to setting you on track to a more positive mood. The movement of your muscles triggers the release of endorphins, which makes us happier. It also helps to reduce levels of the stress hormone cortisol. Your brain can't tell the difference between a real and a fake smile, so even if you're not feeling it inside, give smiling a go.

THE MOST IMPORTANT
THING IS TO ENJOY YOUR
LIFE – TO BE HAPPY –
IT'S ALL THAT MATTERS.

Audrey Hepburn

THE POWER OF "NO"

It's easy to feel you have to do what's asked of you, whether it's to please others, to meet expectations or to maintain a reputation. If you're feeling under pressure, take a moment to define what's necessary to you and don't be afraid to say no to the rest. Politely declining a task with the explanation that you will not be able to complete it in the time needed will not only show your boss that you are

aware of your workload and limits, it will also help alleviate your stress. If you always feel you have to say "yes" then you may be left with too much work. Then you would have the added pressure of finishing tasks late, of not completing them to the desired quality or of having to work additional hours to complete them. This is easy to avoid: just keep an awareness of what you need to do, and say "no" if you need to.

I WILL BE CALM.
I WILL BE MISTRESS
OF MYSELF.

Jane Austen

CHANGE YOUR THOUGHTS
AND YOU CHANGE
YOUR WORLD.

Norman Vincent Peale

TREAT YOURSELF!

Sometimes all you need to give yourself the confidence to face the day is a shift to a more positive mindset. So, if you're feeling tense or anxious, give your mood a boost by giving yourself something to look forward to. There are plenty of small things you can incorporate into everyday life: putting fresh sheets on your bed; making time to watch an episode of a TV programme or your favourite film;

cooking your favourite meal; catching up with a friend; having a tasty treat; having a long bubble bath; going for a stroll in the sunshine; or going to a friend's house for dinner. With something small to lift your spirits and look forward to you'll be in a much better position to deal with the stresses of the day.

BE GLAD OF LIFE BECAUSE
IT GIVES YOU THE CHANCE
TO LOVE, TO WORK,
TO PLAY, AND TO LOOK
UP AT THE STARS.

Henry Van Dyke

FORGET THE PAST
AND LIVE THE
PRESENT HOUR.

Sarah Knowles Bolton

SET A GOAL

Make a resolution, or set yourself an aim to achieve. Our feelings of stress often stem from feeling unfulfilled and unfocused; by setting goals you can gain a sense of clarity and prioritize what is important in your life. Whether your goal is big or small, and whether it's to do with work, your health or your hobbies, having something to work toward will give you focus and, when you achieve it, satisfaction.

ACCEPT WHAT IS, LET GO OF WHAT WAS AND HAVE FAITH IN WHAT WILL BE.

Sonia Ricotti

FIND POSITIVES IN NEGATIVES

Remaining calm and keeping your worries at bay is usually down to how you are able to handle different situations. When something difficult or unexpected happens, it's a natural reaction to feel tense or to let negative feelings take over. Next time this happens, try to find a positive within the situation. This can be hard at first, especially in situations that have a strong and lasting effect on your life.

But finding even a small positive will make the situation easier to deal with. Perhaps you have lost your job, but the positive is that now you can retrain for the career you always wanted. Maybe a relationship has ended; the positive here is that now you're free to find someone more suited to you. Finding the silver lining is not always an easy thing to do, but it's a skill that will greatly help you remain calm and collected.

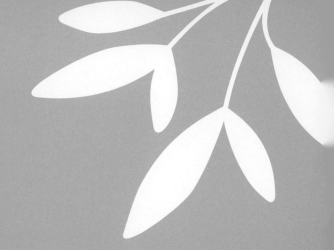

YOU CAN'T CALM THE
STORM, SO STOP TRYING.
WHAT YOU CAN DO IS
CALM YOURSELF. THE
STORM WILL PASS.

Timber Hawkeye

HE WHO
IS CONTENTED
IS RICH.

Lao Tzu

STEP BACK

When we're facing a problem, it often feels like the be-all and end-all, and it's easy for everything else in life to become eclipsed. If you're feeling this way, try taking a step back and looking at the bigger picture. Ask yourself if what you're worried about will matter in a week, a month or a year. Quite often, the answer is no! Adjusting your perspective in this way can help to take the edge off the things that worry you and give you greater peace of mind.

IN THE MADNESS,
YOU HAVE TO
FIND CALM.

Lupita Nyong'o

KEEP YOUR FEELINGS YOUR OWN

A cold isn't the only thing you can catch from other people – stress can also be contagious. We absorb it without realizing too. Studies have shown that even just observing someone who is stressed can have an effect on your own nervous system, whether it's at home or in the workplace. But there are things you can do to counter the effects of second-hand stress. In the same way that your body uses antibodies to combat illness, you can use positivity. If a colleague is talking about work or personal problems, try to say something positive about the subject or offer them advice. If they carry on, perhaps offer to go and make a hot drink to defuse the situation. If you cannot walk away, be aware of your own mood – make sure you stay positive and try your best not to adopt your colleague's mindset.

A MAN OF MEDITATION IS HAPPY, NOT FOR AN HOUR, OR A DAY, BUT QUITE ROUND THE CIRCLE OF ALL HIS YEARS.

Isaac Taylor

WORRY PRETENDS
TO BE NECESSARY
BUT SERVES NO
USEFUL PURPOSE.

Eckhart Tolle

BE OPEN TO CHANGE

Everything is easier with an open mind. If you find the prospect of change daunting, allow your thoughts to be flexible. It's easy to spend a lot of time worrying about things that never happen, so try letting circumstances unfold without dwelling on the outcome. Trust that you will be able to deal with whatever happens, when it happens – and not before.

A CLOUDY DAY IS NO MATCH FOR A SUNNY DISPOSITION.

William Arthur Ward

DON'T BE AFRAID TO CRY

If you need to cry, then let it out! It's often our gut reaction to try to hold tears back, but crying is a healthy and perfectly natural reaction. As well as being a way to release stress and tension, it means that you're acknowledging and confronting your feelings instead of bottling them up and pushing them away, which is always a healthier way to deal with them.

Tears aren't just a way of expressing your emotions either – they also have health benefits, as they help to cleanse the body of the chemicals that raise cortisol, the stress hormone. So, if you're particularly stressed and feel the urge to cry, that's your body's way of trying to make you feel better. Shutting the door and letting it all out will release your tension and help you feel ready to face the world again.

FEAR CANNOT BE
BANISHED, BUT IT CAN BE
CALM AND WITHOUT PANIC;
IT CAN BE MITIGATED BY
REASON AND EVALUATION.

Vannevar Bush

DON'T HURRY,
DON'T WORRY.
AND BE SURE TO
SMELL THE FLOWERS
ALONG THE WAY.

Walter Hagen

ALWAYS BE PREPARED

If there's a daunting event on the horizon, resist the urge to put it out of your mind. Although this kind of coping method can be comforting short term, when the event rolls around you'll be much more stressed than you need to be. Instead, confront the thing that's causing you concern and deal with it by preparing. Give yourself enough time to think about it and approach it logically. For instance, if you have to take a test, draw up a

revision timetable. If you're worried about a presentation at work, practise what you will say beforehand – on your own or in front of a friend – or ask someone to present with you. If you're uneasy about a social event, think about some conversation starters you could use or ask someone you know to go with you. When you feel prepared for what lies ahead and equipped to handle your situation you will feel much more relaxed.

WITHOUT ACCEPTING
THE FACT THAT
EVERYTHING CHANGES,
WE CANNOT FIND
PERFECT COMPOSURE.

Shunryū Suzuki

PEACE. IT DOES NOT MEAN TO BE IN A PLACE WHERE THERE IS NO TROUBLE, NOISE, OR HARD WORK. IT MEANS TO BE IN THE MIDST OF THOSE THINGS AND STILL BE CALM IN YOUR HEART.

Lady Gaga

SOMETIMES THE BIGGEST
ONES ARE IN OUR HEAD
– THE SABOTEURS THAT
TELL US WE CAN'T.

Lupita Nyong'o on obstacles

YOU HAVE TO TAKE CARE OF YOURSELF, YOUR BODY, YOUR MIND, TAKE CARE OF YOUR SOUL – BE YOUR OWN KEEPER.

Jennifer Lopez

FIND SUPPORT

If you're having trouble bringing your stress and anxiety under control, you may find joining a support group helpful. Search online for groups in your local area, and you will get the opportunity to talk to people who are experiencing similar difficulties to you. Mind, a mental health charity in the UK, and Mental Health America are also excellent resources that offer help and advice. If you're still having difficulty with unwanted thoughts and feelings,

it might be worth considering CBT – cognitive behavioural therapy. CBT is a form of psychotherapy that helps you to focus on replacing negative thoughts and behaviour with a more positive mindset. The practice works on the principle that you can change your negative thought patterns in increments by focusing on the present and finding practical ways to improve your outlook. With gradual progress, eventually you will alter the way you think and behave.

THINGS CAN HAPPEN
TO YOU BUT THEY
DON'T HAVE TO HAPPEN
TO YOUR SOUL.

Jennifer Lawrence

REMAIN CALM, SERENE, ALWAYS IN COMMAND OF YOURSELF. YOU WILL THEN FIND OUT HOW EASY IT IS TO GET ALONG.

Paramahansa Yogananda

CALM FOR EVERYONE

Whatever the situation, being calm is something that everybody can achieve. We are all different; although what works for someone else might not work for you, there are so many things you can do to bring yourself a sense of peace – both big and small – that there really is something for everyone. You just need to find the techniques and practices that benefit you. Hopefully, this little book will have helped you to make the first steps toward a calmer and happier life.

WHATEVER YOU'RE WORRIED ABOUT, YOU'RE BIGGER THAN THE WORRIES.

John Green

Have you enjoyed this book? If so, find us on Facebook at **Summersdale Publishers**, on Twitter at **@Summersdale** and on Instagram at **@summersdalebooks** and get in touch. We'd love to hear from you!

www.summersdale.com